THE LAST COWBOY

CD GREENE

I won't argue with you whether the Wild Horse and Burro Protection Act passed by Congress December 18, 1971 was a good or bad thing. I do know and like my Dad said they took the last truly free thing that any man could just go take if he was good enough and put them under government control. Before that the government didn't control the wild horses, neither did we, but we captured some of them.

I don't care if my book is politically correct I could care less if it is grammatically correct as long as its factually correct.

1

HORSES

I just can't remember a time our lives didn't involve horses. From my very first memories we had horses and from the time I can first remember Dad was sittin me on a Shetland pony and holdin on to me. As I got older and if the pony was the least bit gentle, he would strap me to a pony ring saddle and turn us loose out in the front yard. From there I and my cousin would ride our ponies so they could be used in our pony ring that my uncle and cousin traveled with over the summer fair and county fairs and rodeos to make a few dollars. From there it was 4-H clubs saddle clubs game days playdays the Oregon State Fair. Dad kept bringin horses home and I kept ridin 'em out whether it was chasin cows trail ridin or swimmin in the river as long as they did what I wanted we got along fine.

Later on Dad brought home a big bay quarterhorse called Rattler for me to work cattle on. Well I threw a saddle on him and bridled him up and went to see what he could do. He went to throwin his head and actin stupid and I thought great Dad brought home another knot head for me to ride the kinks out of. But since Dad knew a lot more than I did he went and got another headstall with a roller bit in it and slipped it over Rattlers head.

Rattler went to rollin that Roller with his tongue and now we knew how he got his name. He put his head down and was ready to go to work. We cut out cows and roped calves off of him for years. In fact when we went after the wild ones Dad was still ridin ol Rattler. When we picked our horses for out on the desert they were mostly quarterhorses except for me. I picked out a couple of Appaloosas I liked Appys out on the desert. When they had decent wind and we could cover a lot of miles in a day.

BLOOD

I look out the window of our Ranch house looken out over the corrals and see my granddaughter standing on top of my saddle horse. I've told her not to but she doesn't listen any better than when I was her age.

It must RUN in the blood.

I remember her mother, my daughter helping us gather cattle on Klamath Marsh getting bucked off and getting back on to help us finish. Later in town we learned she had a broken collarbone.

It must RUN in the blood.

At night lookin at the pictures of all the horses another of my daughters rode and all the fun we had.

It must RUN in the blood.

I remember my younger brother bottle feedin that knot head bay colt we got off the desert and raisen it up till it could eat on its own

It must RUN in the blood

My cousin was a team Roper that qualified for the senior National Finals Rodeo.

It must RUN in the blood.

My uncle who lost his left hand in the hay fields in South Dakota and could still rope better than most cowboys with two hands.

It must RUN in the blood.

Another uncle who supported his family and raised his four kids skidded logs with horses for Oregon State University in the Black Rock Area outside of Falls City, OR.

It must RUN in the blood

In the morning seen my Dad crow hoppin across the pasture on his big black quarter horse Nina, Dad never cared for a horse much if it didn't have some spirit.

It must RUN in the blood

My grandfather moved logs at the Susanville Sawmill in Susanville, CA. with his team of horses.

It must RUN in the blood

Sittin on the front porch with my grandmother who lived to be ninety-eight and her tellen me you know the reason I married your grandfather was because he rode the best horse in the county.

You bet it RUNs in the blood.

2

THE LAST COWBOY

I rolled out of bed one early, bright summer morning at my Dads not so subtle urging. I had just graduated from McNary High School in Keizer Oregon a suburb of Salem Oregon. Not exactly cowboy country but we were within twenty miles of the St. Paul Rodeo and the Molalla Buckaroos both held each year on the fourth of July we went every year sometimes to St. Paul in the afternoon and Molalla in the evening.

I wasn't a cowboy yet i just thought I was I was raised by a cowboy on a twenty seven acre farm with cattle and horses so it fell to me and my cousin to break the ponies for our Pony Ring which my uncle and cousin ran for a couple years until my Dad saw the liability of putting young children on half broke ponies when the Rodeo decides to start there fireworks show early without telling us. Sidenote Shetland ponies are the meanest critters on earth. As I got older Dad bought me different horses to ride none broke to ride. If I wanted to ride there was one way get on and hold on

But enough about me this morning my Dad was about to take me on an adventure an adventure that I was to dumb to appreciate till years later. and believe me we sure didn't do it for the money.

Don Greene, 1971

3

THE COWBOYS

DON GREENE: RAMROD

My Dad was a cowboy from the word go, but he had to make a living and riding colts and feeding somebody else's cows wasn't going to work. He left Paisley, Oregon — population less than a hundred — with a high school diploma and no money. He ended up owning a road construction company that built state highways and forest service roads. He logged, built a golf course, a mobile home park, owned a restaurant and lounge, a pony ring, but no matter what he did he wore his hat and boots every day 'cause he was a cowboy first. He must have done pretty good financially on his last road job to bankroll our adventure out on the desert.

He tried to explain to me one night why we were chasing wild horses and he told me, *"You know wild horses are the last thing a man can just go take if he's man enough. Nobody owns them, nobody can stop us. They run free on government land and we can just take them if we're good enough."*

Whether we did this because my Dad wanted to relive his

younger days or because he wanted me and my brother to experience what he had, I don't know, but I will be forever grateful.

Roy Ousley, 1971

ROY OUSLEY

COWBOY AND CAMP COOK

Roy, like my Dad, was a cowboy first and a catskinner to make a living. When my Dad told Roy about his plan to run wild horses in the Steens Mountains, Roy was all in. Roy was from Burns and had worked on ranches south of Burns and knew a lot about desert horses. No wages, just expenses, but you didn't have to ask Roy twice.

Roy hauled his Airstream trailer in for us to camp in. For breakfast we usually got two eggs, toast, maybe a couple slices of bacon– thick cut bacon that had to hold us till we got back to camp. Roy also brought the biggest pot I have ever seen. He would fill it with red beans and water and that was dinner until it was gone. So, four cowboys ride hard all day, at night sleep in an Airstream trailer — what could possibly go wrong? Well, when the beans were gone, Roy would take a whole canned chicken, throw it in the pot and fill it with water and noodles. Now you might think that doesn't sound all that great, but after you ride twenty, twenty-five miles a day you might think different.

Roy hauled in two horses off a ranch south of Burns — one was a lanky palomino that was Roy's favorite, and the other was Ol' Red, a big ugly sorrel horse. Big head, big hooves, but he could fly like the wind. The idea was Roy would alternate horses one day working, the next day resting, but if his palomino had an easy day, I would beg Roy to let me ride Ol' Red. Ol' Red was fast and sure-footed and made our valley horses look like plow horses. He was the only horse we had that could put me in a bunch.

Another thing I remember is among the bunches we got in, two branded horses that Dad had to deal with. Anyway, Roy knew if you get a branded gelding in with a bunch, he belongs to somebody else off a ranch somewhere. Roy said he thought he saw saddle marks on him and was going to try to ride him. Now I'm not dumb enough to take anything away from professional cowboys that ride the rodeo circuit for a living — they're some of the best in the world — but there's something special about an old cowboy that will crawl on a strange horse out on the desert, no prize money, no cheers from the crowd, and over a hundred miles from the nearest hospital.

Roy got on him and rode him just because he could. Now that's a cowboy. Roy rode him and tried to use him to chase the wild ones. *Brownie* rode okay, but when you got off after a bunch he took the bit and stuck his jaw straight out and you couldn't do anything with him, and just had to ride him till he ran himself out. I think Roy was a better cowboy than he was a cook, but I kept that opinion to myself.

Curt Greene and Don Greene, 1971

CURT GREENE

AND THE SAN FRANCISCO GIANTS

I remember out on the desert being the only one who didn't get to go to town. Roy got to go because he was Dad's buddy, and Orrin got to go because he was the youngest. I got to stay in camp and feed horses. Eighteen years old out on the desert — no TV, no girls, no beer, nothin'.

But at night, when the sky was clear and you could reach up and touch the stars, I'd get my San Francisco Giants games out of the Bay Area on KAGO AM. They came in crystal clear and helped me maintain my sanity that and an occasional shower at an old artesian well three or four miles from camp.

You know there is a certain feeling of freedom when you stand naked on the desert under a pipe coming out of the ground, cold artesian water pouring over your head? That's freedom.

Ol' Red was the only horse I ever rode that could put me in amongst a bunch of wild ones, our valley horses couldn't come close. But I remember Ol' Red jumping rocks and flying over sagebrush and putting me right along beside one where I could reach out and slap them on the rump. I don't know of any other feeling like running flat out with the wild ones. Now I'm the last cowboy standing, the last one to tell the tale — the others have passed on.

Orrin Greene, 1971

ORRIN GREENE

THE YOUNGEST COWBOY

What do you say about your younger brother? He was either twelve or thirteen and tried to do things like we did and I will give him this — he didn't complain much. He could ride, and Dad had him on a good horse, and I think he even turned a bunch once or twice.

I remember Dad tellen me when they were at the feed store, and Orrin came up to the counter with a bottle and a bag of milk replacer. So Dad paid for it. Orrin had decided he wanted to try to bottle-feed one of the colts that had followed us into camp. Those colts are tough and they want to live, so he took to being bottle-fed and Orrin raised him until he could eat on his own.

I don't remember what he did with that horse, but I do remember him raising it. Later in life Orrin got his horsepower from motorcycles rather than horses.

Well, we each live our own life.

I realized a couple months ago after my brother passed that I was the last cowboy left that had legally captured wild horses on the Oregon desert, and if the story was going to be told, it was up to me to tell it.

BERNELL GREENE

MY MOTHER

What kind of woman would let her husband take her sons out on the desert to chase wild horses for months at a time.

A very special woman that's what kind. I only mention my Mom because I need to acknowledge how this film was made and preserved. My Dad might have been a cowboy but he knew the power of knowledge so us kids had encyclopedias a new electric typewriter and the latest and greatest in home movie camera and projector and that's what Mom let us take out on the desert to film some of our adventures up til that time the only movie film I had seen was a 35mm You— threaded in a projector. Well I don't know what this technology was called I'm sure it was a forerunner of VHS cause the salesman kept saying over and over again you don't ever touch the film. The film was in a clear plastic cartridge that went in the camera and you could take the cartridge out and put it in the projector to show it and that's what I did. Sometime later I realized that technology was going away or maybe the projector quit working so I had it transferred to VHS and had three copies made. Then after DVDs came out I had two copies made from the VHS tape. Whether it was blind luck or divine intervention I was able to preserve our piece of history until I finally realized I had something unique.

Something special a one of a kind that can never be duplicated and I hope I can share it with you. But I digress I've always wanted to say that. Let's get back to the horses.

4

THE INDIANS

Yes I call them Indians because thats what they call themselves. I may not be politically correct, but neither are they. One of my friends was a bullrider and pound for pound one of the toughest men I ever met. I just realized I didn't say Indian friend maybe thats because thats not the way I think, a friend is a friend. Indians have a great sense of humor in fact, if more of the world had their sense of humor it would be a better place. Like when one of my, ok i'll say it, Indian friends asked me who my favorite football team was and I proudly said the Raiders. So in turn I asked him who his favorite team was and he looked at me like I was stupid, and said "the Redskins, who did you think?" and cracked up laughing. See what I mean?

Anyway we turned off highway ninety-seven by Thunderbeast Park and headed out towards the marsh. Dad had eighty acres out there where we ran cattle it was about half meadow and half lodgepole timber. lodgepole timber is kind of a scrub pine if its not to limby it makes good corral poles.

Well we found the truck Dads Fifty-Seven Mack with a lowboy trailer and two Indians loading lodgepoles. Dad asked them where Gordon was and they said they didn't know. Gordon had dropped them off told them what to do and took off. Dad wasn't too happy, but told the Indians we'd help finish loading the truck and maybe Gordon would show up. Gordon was the son of the chief of the Paiute Indians around McDermott Nevada. Gordon ran a cat scraper on my Dads last road construction job and the one I figured was responsible for what I would be doing the next few months of my life. Gordon and some of the Indians from around McDermott had been capturing wild horses up in the Steens Mountains south of Burns Oregon. Gordon said the problem they had was they only built one corral and had to haul out the horses everytime they got a bunch in. well Gordon knew Dad had a truck and some lodgepole timber. So Gordon told Dad if he would haul a load of lodgepole out on the desert and help build a holding corral he would let us run wild horses with them. He didn't have to ask twice my Dad was cowboy from the word go and he didn't think twice he was ready to go and so was I, I guess.

When Gordon finally showed up he had went to town and got drunk after he dropped the other two Indians off on the marsh. How he drove back I have no idea he couldn't hardly stand up, but Gordon wanted to show Dad he could work and fired up one of the chainsaws. He started trying to cut off the small end of the logs hanging off the end of the lowboy trailer. After Gordon hit the back of the trailer a few times with the chainsaw one of the Indians took it away from him and told him to sit down and stay out of the way. But Gordon wanted to help and as we worked to tie down the load with chains and binders he continued to get in the way. In spite of all of Gordons help we were loaded and ready to head to Burns the two Indians got in their pickup and took off, then it dawned on me there were three of us and only two seats in the truck. Dad drove the truck Gordon passed out in the other seat that left me jammed on the floor between Gordon and the shifters for the truck. Not a fun trip.

A day or two later Gordon showed up with our crew the two Indians that cut the lodgepole, and three more he got out of the local jail. The sheriff would release them if Gordon told him he was taking them out on the desert to work. One of them was one of the biggest Indians I've ever seen I'm guessin six three six four and well over two hundred fifty pounds. Dad said we needed to start unloading the truck so I jumped up on the trailer where the light stuff was and the big Indian went to the heavy ends. I didn't know any of their names except Gordon, but I soon caught on the other Indians called this big Indian Baby they did I didn't. We started lifting lodgepole logs and throwing them off the trailer. After we unloaded about half the load I was ready for a break. But Baby just kept bendin over and picken em up do you think my eighteen year old smartness would let him outwork me we unloaded that whole load without stopping and I about fell off the trailer. So what does Baby do he walks over picks up a shovel and starts digging post holes. Baby dug two postholes for every one I dug and I just had to live with it. He was the better man that day and my Dad got a good laugh outta it.

I don't remember much about chasing the wild ones with the Indians they would take us out on a stand and tell us to wait until they brought the horses off the top so the first day we waited about six to eight hours no horses. Second day same thing Dad said he saw a bunch of horses that came off the top but he got them nowhere near the corral. You learn something about patience when your off your horse sittin on a rock out on the desert for hour after hour waiting for something to happen.

We thought the Indians knew about chasing wild horses, and I'm sure they knew some, but where they located the corral was not one of them. They built the corral at the foot of a hill, that had a V shaped notch at the top the idea was to run the horses thru the V and then force them downhill into the corral They thought if we had the high ground we could push them down into the corral.

Two mistakes one when a bunch of horses hit the V and could see the other side they could see both corrals our camp our pickups our trailers and they wanted no part of it back they came and we only pushed a bunch in when we got lucky Second mistake was to think you could force a wild horse into a corral good luck

Anybody that tries to tell you what a wild horse will do doesn't know what a wild horse will do.

Years later I did talk to a cowboy who was contracted by the BLM to gather wild horses. He told me they put their corrals, he called them traps on an uphill grade so the horses were in the wings or maybe even in the trap before they realized it. Made sense to me.

Anyway the second night the last night with the Indians we were sitting around a campfire and I got a taste of Indian humor. That day a baby colt got separated from a bunch and followed Baby's horse back to camp. Around the campfire I heard the other Indians teasing Baby, oh Baby big horse hunter Baby show us how to catch horses Baby catch wild horse big horse hunter. It went on and on and it was funny but there was no way I was dumb enough to laugh at somebody that big.

A cold night and a warm beer, 1970.

Around the campfire that night they offered me a Rhinelander beer. Cheap beer but man did it taste good and I felt pretty good knowing they liked me enough to part with a beer. I drank my beer and listened to them tease Baby and enjoyed my last night on the desert with the Indians in the morning they were gone. Dad had tried several times to get them to show us how to get on top. No such luck. Now they were gone and we were on our own I think Dad liked that.

Grandview, Idaho, 1970

5

THE BASQUES

We got in the first and only bunch of horses that year in the spring of nineteen seventy. When we went to haul out we had to rent a truck because Dad's truck was broke down. So we rented a truck and hauled a load to a packing plant in Grandview, Idaho. We threw a canvas top on the truck and began trying to load. Wild horses don't want to be loaded on a truck and it took us most of a day to get them loaded. We drove to Grandview.

The owner of the truck, Roy, and me — at least Roy shared the seat with me — arrived late in the afternoon. We went to the packing plant manager's office and he had to send out some Basque workers who didn't speak English to help us unload. They had little pop whips, and when we opened the door they headed in. Roy had to stop them, in fact he had to wrestle with them a bit before they realized not to go in the truck.

Roy and I got some sticks and poked at 'em and got them moving enough one got pushed and fell; out then they all came. When they hit the ground they were mad, and one big bay stud stood on his hind legs and chomped down on a four-by-four that went over the scales.

You should have seen the looks on those Basques' faces — they realized if they would have went in that truck they wouldn't have come out. They tried to talk to us and I'm sure there was a "thank you" in there somewhere, and we headed home. Well now, we've captured a bunch of wild horses about a dozen out of the Steens Mountains Now it's time to go back to work for a while, the summer of 1970 we built 6 ½ miles of logging access road for the forest service, then in the fall we went back out on the desert and built reservoirs for the BLM to capture and store natural runoff from the snowmelt in the mountains to provide water for wildlife and livestock. Then we holed up for the rest of the winter and got ready for the next trip into the Steens. All we had to do was wait for the dirt roads into horse camp to dry enough to get our pickups in and it was time for our second round of catching the wild ones.

Lookin for the way on top, 1971

6

THE HORSES

I remember sitting at the base of the Steens Mountains looking up and wondering how these wild ones got up and down. Roy was trying to convince Dad he saw horses coming down this notch in the side of the hill. I had my doubts there were boulders as big as a school bus and it was a jumble of rock. Dad said he didn't think a billy goat could go down it. But Roy was adamant he saw horses come out of that notch. Turns out neither of them was right. Dad saw a little canyon to the right of the notch with a little game trail going up it and thought that was maybe how they traveled up and down from on top.

So Dad and I headed up the canyon and left Roy and Orrin below in case we kicked any horses off. We followed that trail up the canyon. Sometimes we had to walk our horses and sometimes I didn't even want to look down and Dad reminded me if my horse went over to let go of the reins. Afternoon our canyon turned into a ravine and turned north as we came up to the edge to look we could see a bunch of horses heading toward the north. Dad said if we stayed in the ravine and went north we could probably come up on the other side of them. So we worked our way north then turned west on the far side of a little hill.

As we crested the top of the hill we came face to face with a bunch of wild ones. A stud snorted and took off and the race was on. Dad said he would stay to the east to try to push them off and I should follow them south. Well since I was on a valley horse I did my best to keep up and follow their dust. Pretty soon I jumped more bunches and before long had probably close to a hundred head of horses on the move most going in front of me, but some cutting back behind me. I followed a bunch and watched them go right off the side of the mountain and disappear. I got off my horse to take a look — the horses were gone, but I followed their trail right to the edge and over. I couldn't believe it they had worn a zig zag trail down the mountain and it was right next to the notch Roy said he saw horses come out of. You couldn't see it from the basin floor, but it was there and it zig zagged way back and forth all the way down the mountain. I had no idea where my Dad was and he told me to follow the horses so I got off my horse and headed down the trail. It took me a couple of hours to work my way down that trail. I headed towards camp and picked my brother up along the way. When we got back it was dark we were just headed in the wings. I told Orrin "I think I hear horses ahead of us." It's so quiet out on the desert you can hear a hoof click on rock or sense movement. We couldn't see them but I knew they were there.

I carried my grandpa's four-ten shotgun and I told Orrin I was going to shoot and try to scare the horses into the corral so I pulled my horse's head away. I laid that shotgun out there and just as I pulled the trigger my horse jumped back to look and it went off right between his ears. I threw the shotgun grabbed leather and made the ride of my young life. I didn't want to get piled on those rocks.

Roy was at the camp waiting but there was no sign of Dad. This was one of the few times in my life when I worried about my Dad. He always made it no matter what, but when it got to be midnight and he wasn't back I was ready to go start lookin. Roy convinced me we couldn't do anything in the dark so we waited. Sometime after two my Dad came in pretty well wore out. He didn't follow the horses off like I did so he had to pick his way back down the canyon. I'm still not sure how he made it back down but was glad he did.

I don't remember too much of the everyday chasen — sometimes we got skunked and sometimes we captured a bunch. After we had captured over ninety head out of the Steens Dad called a halt. Now we needed to figure out what to do with them.

A FOOTNOTE TO THE HORSES

When you watch the movie you will see a really old stud that ran in with a bunch. We called him Father Time. He ran in like a young stud and snorted and pawed the ground, but after fighting the other studs all night he was done in. In fact, it took us about half a day just to get him out of the corral and close the gate. We expected to find his carcass the next day in the wings of the corral, but on a good note he was gone — we never found a trace of him. He must have made it back on top with the wild ones because that's what he was, a wild one.

7

WILD HORSE ANNIE

We captured horses in the Steens mountains in the spring of nineteen seventy and seventy-one just before it was made illegal by the wild horse and burro protection act passed by congress and signed by President Richard Nixon in December of nineteen seventy-one. I won't argue with you whether the wild horse and burro protection act was a good thing or a bad thing, I do know and like my Dad said they took the last truly free thing that any man could just go take; if he was man enough and put it under government control. Before that the government didn't control the wild horses, neither did we, but we did capture some of them. I won't argue against the wild horse and burro act, but it does chafe me how it was passed. It was prompted by a Eugene OR schoolteacher eventually nicknamed Wild Horse Annie. Well I don't know if she ever saw horses in the wild, but I would bet my last dime she never captured one or broke it to ride but I did. She got the school kids to start a letter writing campaign to Congress and wrote an article published in Readers Digest that was mostly untrue. In her imagination she fancied that there was only one stud to a bunch well please tell me what happened to the other studs. If you watch the movie you will see that the bunches are roughly half studs and half mares. Yes you will sometimes see two or three old studs running together that have been whipped out of the bunch, but the truth is there population I think is similar to humans or domestic horses part male part female and yes studs have been fighting over mares just like men have been fighting over women forever. Another thing that wasn't true was when a bunch is pushed the one magnificent stud of her imagination would lead the bunch from danger. Well I know when I pushed a bunch if there was a dominant mare she was just as apt to take the lead and run flat out. I know I was there. If I have to come down on one side or the other of the protection act I would vote in favor of it not based on somebody's romantic fantasy but based on fact. I do think the wild horses are special they're magnificent and they do deserve to be protected.

Wild Ones, 1971

8

THE HORSES

Now that we had ninety head of wild ones what do we do with 'em. Dad had some property on Klamath Marsh, in Klamath County Oregon there was pasture and some good corrals so we hauled them there. We worked the horses there cuttin some of the studs and branding horses. As you see we're old school no electric branding iron here, just a fire and a branding iron just like it should be done. Now a side note on Dad's branding iron it was made in Paisley, Oregon by the local blacksmith. My Dad's initials were DV for Donald Vernon but when we went to pick up the branding iron they had made it VD instead of DV. Since Dad didn't have the five dollars to have the brand remade our brand has been VD on the right hip for almost a hundred years. But yes like Dylan I went electric after Dad passed.

Well we kept the horses in the corral till Dad got tired of buying hay and he and Roy decided to turn them out on pasture to which I told them you'll never see them again. Roy explained to me these were desert horses and they'd never seen a river and they wouldn't cross the Williamson. Well the first time we went out to gather them they jumped in the river and looked like a bunch of ducks swimming to the other side. Roy was wrong about the wild ones again. Well for Dad and Roy it was a blessing they got to start a new adventure, one that did not include me. The wild ones were out on approximately seven thousand private acres and over forty thousand of Klamath Marsh National Wildlife Refuge. Well it gave Dad and Roy another roundup one that would take all summer and into fall. In fact the last couple of times they gathered them they chased them on snowmobiles. Can you imagine two old fart cowboys chasing wild horses on the Klamath Marsh on snowmobiles. Well they did and according to there count they got all of them back except one of which they never found a trace.

The next stop for the horses was Hubbard Oregon about twenty miles north of Keizer where we lived. Dad rented some corrals and pens to keep the horses in. Our bunch was smaller now we had lost one sold some and given some away to any cowboy who thought he was good enough to break one and some did. Now we still had a nice bunch of horses and Dad decided we should try to start a buckin string for rodeos. We started out hauling some horses to the Linn Benton County Fairgrounds where kids from the Oregon State Rodeo Club in Corvallis would pay us five dollars a ride but by some . Well we weren't gonna get rich at five dollars a ride, but boy some of those horses could really buck. I remember my Dad contacted the biggest stock contractor in Oregon and they agreed to try three of them. Dad hauled them down there and they turned 'em out with there horses and the wild ones headed for the high country and it took the stock contractor all summer to get them back in. They called my Dad when they got them back in and said they were going to try them at the Portland International Rodeo one of the last of the year, well they only tried one; a big sorrel but the cowboy got a seventy three on him and I've seen a lot worse scores than that. The next day the stock contractor called Dad and said they weren't interested they were just to hard to handle. Well I would think it would be a hard thing for a cowboy to admit a horse was to hard to handle, but I understood they traveled year round and had to have horses that were easy to load and take care of. So they told Dad they were up at the stockyards in

Portland and they would meet us at about nine am the next day. Well we hooked on to our Circle J three horse trailer and headed to Portland. When we got there nobody met us and we found our horses in a field with their Rodeo Bulls. I told Dad I didn't want those horses that bad so we walked around about an hour. My Dad is not a patient man.

So finally he convinced me the bulls were in the far end of the field and I should try to work the horses up to the pens. Why me? was my first question to which Dad explained I was the fastest. Made sense to me I guess. I worked our horses into the pens and we haltered them and loaded 'em into our horse trailer. 'Bout that time a couple big stock trucks rolled in and came to a stop in front of our pickup. Their stock foreman jumped down and walked up to us. He looked at us and he looked at our trailer and he said "Don if you would have told me you and this boy loaded those three horses in that three horse trailer by yourself I'd a called you a liar, but I see it for myself and still don't believe it." So after a little BS and a see ya later we headed back to Keizer. The wild ones got fewer and fewer. We owned horses every day of my life so I don't remember how or when the last wild one was gone, but it closed a chapter in my life. A final thought: if anybody tells you what a wild horse is going to do have a good laugh the only thing I learned about a wild horse is they want to stay wild. Later on Dad got a big envelope from the BLM with all the laws pertaining to wild horses and a contract to fill out and sign if he wanted to gather wild horses for the government. He never filled it out I just don't think he was interested.

Fortunately we never captured anything that looked like this. Photo by: Kelly Rigby

9
KIGER MUSTANGS

Later on I realized some of the horses we had captured were the famous Kiger Mustangs. Now I can tell a filly from a stud, but I didn't know anything about Kiger Mustangs. So I read and studied about them and I hope the information I gathered is accurate it seems right to me. They say the Kiger mustang is a descendant of Spanish horses brought here hundreds of years ago. Kigers are generally medium size horses with some unique color markings. I've been raised around horses all my life, and I know what a buckskin is with a dark mane and tail, but some of the horses we captured were that coloring with a sorrel main and tail only time I'd seen it. The Kiger mustangs exhibit color characteristics known as the dun factor which is also common to the Spanish horses colors of the dun factor can be dun, red dun, grulla (mousy gray) buckskin and other variations. Markings can include a dorsal stripe from mane to tail, zebra stripes on the legs and a darker outline on there hooked ears. They say the less white the stronger the dun factor. I found them to be intelligent with tremendous stamina, they just never seemed to get tired. They say the only place in the world you find Kiger Mustangs in the wild is in the Steens mountains of Eastern Oregon well that's where we found them. They go on to say Kiger Mustangs have never been bred or raised in captivity. Well I think our movie clearly shows that's not true. If you watch the movie and see the horses if they don't look like pictures of Spanish horses I've seen I'll throw in with ya, but you do have to realize they have interbred with desert horses so the breed has changed over the years. When I heard Disney was doing a movie about the Kiger Mustangs I tried to contact them that I had some film of Kiger Mustangs I thought they might want to use as an intro or a trailer but I never heard back from them.

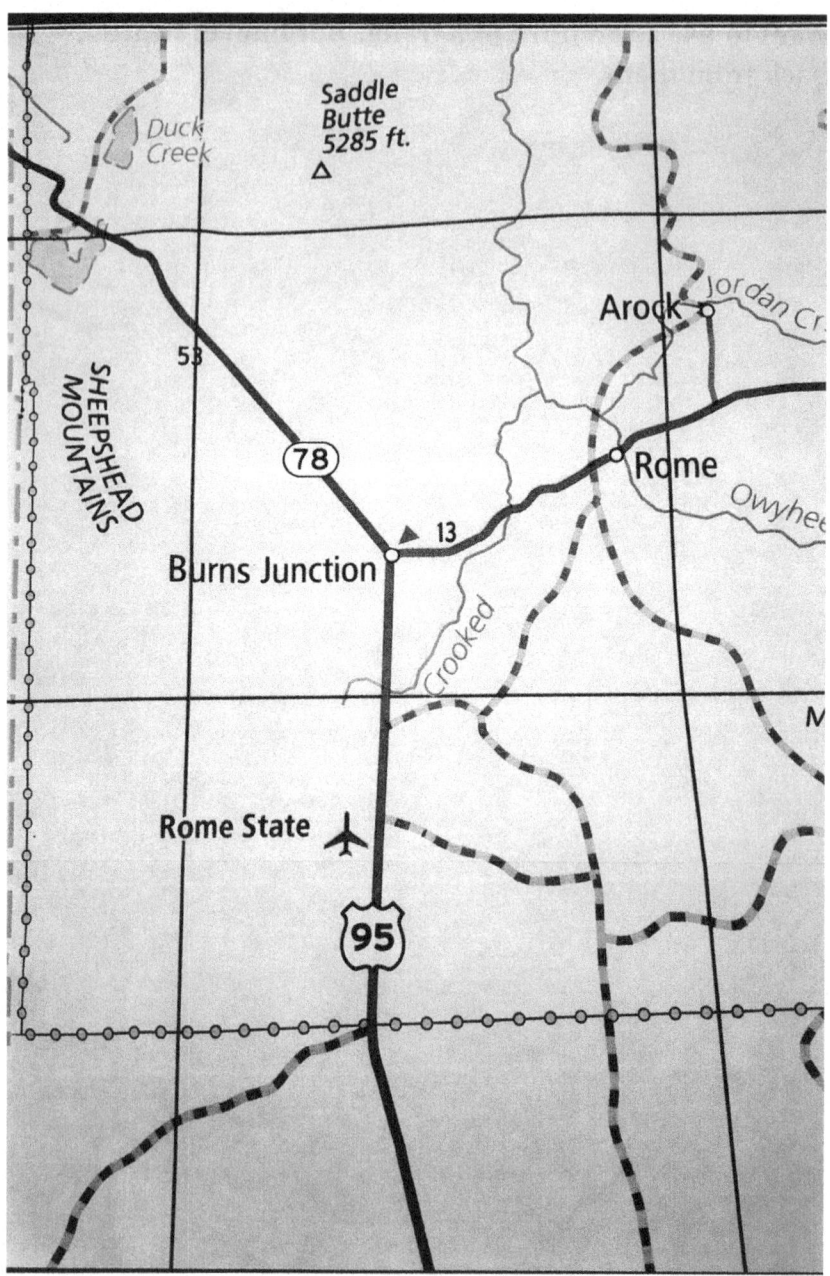

Sheepshead Mountains, circa 1970

10

THE BLM

BUREAU OF LAND MANAGEMENT

The BLM manages and protects wild horses on twenty five million acres across ten western states, but I'm only concerned about how they manage the area where we captured horses in nineteen seventy and nineteen seventy-one. So I decided it was time for a trip to the wild horse holding corrals at Burns OR. I hadn't been there in about fifteen years, but the pens and corrals were pretty much as I remembered. What was different was the horses; they were slightly smaller than I remember and color everywhere. Pintos black and white, brown and white color everywhere.

You notice I said pinto not paint. Paint horses are classified by breeding and color not that some of the desert horses don't show some good breeding, but pintos are classified strictly by color as long as they have large areas of white and another color they can be called pintos and I never saw a pinto in the area where we captured horses. The people at the corrals explained their horses were from the southern loop of the Steens Mountains and a completely different herd from where the Kiger Mustangs roamed.

I had always assumed the wild horses in the Steens Mountains were all about the same boy was I wrong, different areas, different herds, different breeding, different horses. The BLM in Burns manages two areas in southeastern Oregon for wild horses with Spanish mustang characteristics.

The two areas located in the Burns District are known as the Kiger and Riddle Mountain HMAs (Herd Management Areas). The HMA covers almost thirty seven thousand acres and is managed for a herd population of approximately fifty to eighty horses. The Riddle Mountain HMA covers about thirty thousand acres and is managed for a herd of approximately thirty to sixty horses. I'm confused because the holding corrals in Burns are less than one hundred miles from where we captured horses and they don't seem to know too much about the area we were in. Now as I start to get my bearings I realized the road we turned into the Steens Mountains has more than one name that helps a lot. Where we turned there is a state road sign that says Folly Farm Road, but after five miles it's called the Fields Denio highway.

Wild Horses from Souther Loop of the Steen Mountains, Summer 2025

. . .

ANYWAY I EVENTUALLY FOUND OUT THE area we captured horses in is called the Sheepshead Heath Creek HMA and is managed out of the BLM office in Vale OR. In talking to the BLM office in Vale they said they had recently done a gathering in that area and reduced the herd population by several hundred horses leaving best guess about three hundred horses to be managed. When we were there in nineteen seventy one we had guessed that there were between three to four hundred horses in that area, but it was only a guess you could never see them all at one time. Some wild horses can be adopted right at the holding corrals if you meet there requirements, but because of the popularity of the Kiger Mustangs there adoptions are done mostly online. I have included some pictures of the horses from the Burns holding corrals so you can see the complete difference from the horses we captured. I'd like to thank the people of the BLM for their time and information. From my experience and what my opinions are worth I think the BLM does a pretty good job of taking care of one of our national treasures. Like I may have said before the BLM sent my Dad a packet with a contract to gather wild horses in the Steens Mountains. He never returned it we didn't do it for the money.

THE HORSES

THEIR FATE

I know I'll anger a certain group of people when I admit we culled our horses and sent some of the older ones to a packing plant, but how much sleep do they lose about all the cattle and hogs that go to slaughter everyday. Yeah I know horses are different, but the result is the same. We sold them, gave them away to family, broke them to ride in fact a couple of them made dang good saddle horses and we had a buckin string. We never crippled a horse in fact the only one we lost was one we turned out on Klamath Marsh. We're cowboys and we take good care of our horses.

WHO PROTECTS THEM

I get real tired of hearing from college professors, environmental groups, animal right groups about what is best for the wild ones why don't they find somebody that at least knows a little bit about them. Lately I've been hearing about eradicating wild horses in certain areas. I don't remember that in the wild horse and burro protection act. If you're gonna have a fit because I step on some endangered grass out in the wilderness maybe we can keep a few horses in areas where they've roamed for over a hundred years. I don't have all the answers but what about a tax credit to help promote the wild horse adoption program. Why not we have one for everything else. I've heard about a new fertility program that might help control the population that might help. For now there under government control the government is responsible for them and the need to treat them like the national treasure they are.

A LAST THOUGHT

I hope each and everyone of you who reads this can look at one time in your life when you really lived. Whether it was eight seconds on a bull, jumping out of an airplane, something you did on your job, the birth of a child, maybe sometime when you helped someone or that one time when you really lived. Well when I chased the wild ones on the desert I really lived.

THE LAST COWBOY RIDES AWAY

What prompted me to sit down and write this was when my brother died and I realized I was the last one to tell the story, and I realized I had a lot more trail behind me than I had ahead of me. When I sat down to record it this story just poured out of me. I've never experienced anything like that. This is the original draft. I thought about rewriting it, or adding to it, or changing words, but I decided to leave well enough alone. I wanted it to be just like we were sitting on the porch and just telling you the story. I hope you enjoyed sharing my story as much as I did in telling it.

Happy Trails,
And don't tighten the back cinch first.

Made in the USA
Coppell, TX
03 March 2026